DEADLY
DINOSAURS

Collector Card

DEADLY
DINOSAURS

Collector Card

DEADLY
DINOSAURS

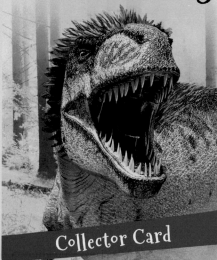

Collector Card

DEADLY
DINOSAURS

Collector Card

Diplodocus

This dinosaur was one of the longest animals that ever lived.

SCORE

LENGTH: 35 m	10
DANGER RATING:	3
FOSSIL RECORD: 6 skeletons plus parts	8
WEIGHT: 25,000 kg	10

Allosaurus

This dinosaur was a killing machine with serrated teeth.

SCORE

LENGTH: 12 m	6
DANGER RATING:	8
FOSSIL RECORD: parts of 48 skeletons	9
WEIGHT: 2000 kg	4

Stegosaurus

The bony plates that run along this dinosaur's spine are very distinctive.

SCORE

LENGTH: 9 m	6
DANGER RATING:	7
FOSSIL RECORD: 80 fossils	6
WEIGHT: 3100 kg	6

Dimorphodon

The first fossils of this dinosaur were found in 1828 by Mary Anning.

SCORE

LENGTH: 1 m	1
DANGER RATING:	2
FOSSIL RECORD: 3 skeletons plus parts	3
WEIGHT: unknown	1

It's all about…

DEADLY
DINOSAURS

KINGFISHER

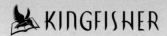

First published 2015 by Kingfisher
an imprint of Pan Macmillan
a division of Macmillan Publishers International Ltd
20 New Wharf Road, London N1 9RR
Associated companies throughout the world
www.panmacmillan.com

Series editor: Sarah Snashall
Series design: Little Red Ant
Adapted from an original text by Claire Llewellyn and Thea Feldman

ISBN 978-0-7534-3889-3

9 8 7 6 5 4 3 2 1

1TR/0415/WKT/UG/128MA

A CIP catalogue record for this book is available from the British Library.

Printed in China

Picture credits
The Publisher would like to thank the following for permission to reproduce their material.
Top = t; Bottom = b; Centre = c; Left = l; Right = r
Pages 2–3, 6–7 & 30–31 Shutterstock/Catmando; 4bl Corbis/Corey Ford; 5cr Shutterstock/
Catmando; 22b Shutterstock/Catmando; 22-23 & 23 Shutterstock/Michael Rosskothen;
24–25 Shutterstock/sdecoret; 25 Shutterstock/miha de; 28 Shutterstock/Jorg Hackemann;
29t Shutterstock/mikeledray; 29b Shutterstock/valda
Cards: Front bl Shutterstock/Elenarts; tr Shutterstock/Jean-Michel Girard; br Shutterstock/
Michael Rosskothen; Back tl & tr Shutterstock/Michael Rosskothen
All other images Kingfisher Artbank.

CONTENTS

For your free audio download go to
http://panmacmillan.com/Deadly Dinosaurs
or goo.gl/uLpvwa
Happy listening!

Ancient reptiles

Dinosaurs were reptiles that lived between about 230 and 65 million years ago. They were the most important land animals of their time.

FACT...

The long stretch of the Earth's early history is split into three eras, or periods: Triassic, Jurassic and Cretaceous.

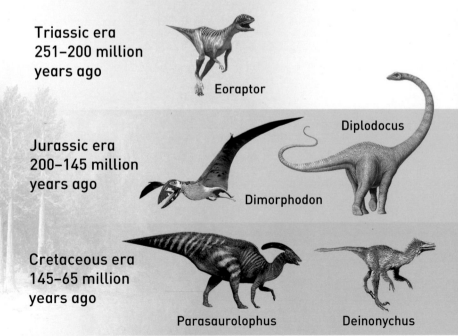

Triassic era
251–200 million years ago

Eoraptor

Jurassic era
200–145 million years ago

Dimorphodon

Diplodocus

Cretaceous era
145–65 million years ago

Parasaurolophus

Deinonychus

Most dinosaurs ate plants, but some were the deadliest meat-eaters the world has ever seen. Some dinosaurs were as long as three houses; others were the size of a chicken.

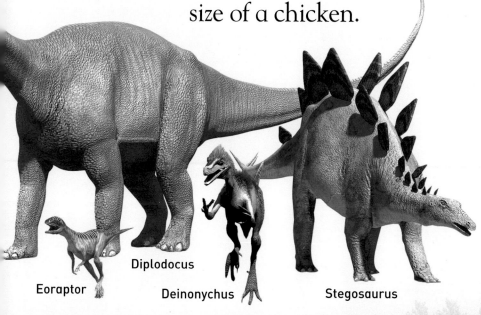

Eoraptor

Diplodocus

Deinonychus

Stegosaurus

Stegosaurus

Allosaurus

Maiasaura

Tyrannosaurus rex

Gentle giant

Diplodocus was huge! It had a big body, strong legs, a long neck, a long tail but only a small head.

FACT...

Diplodocus swallowed stones to help crush the food in its stomach.

Ferns were food for Diplodocus and other plant-eaters.

Diplodocus fed on bushes and trees, tearing off leaves with its teeth. Diplodocus was so massive that it had to eat all the time just to stay alive.

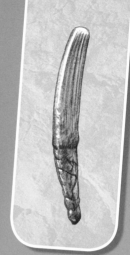

Diplodocus had teeth like this.

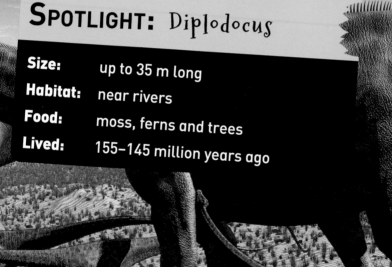

SPOTLIGHT: Diplodocus

Size:	up to 35 m long
Habitat:	near rivers
Food:	moss, ferns and trees
Lived:	155–145 million years ago

Killing machine

Allosaurus was an excellent hunter. It was one of the deadliest killers of all time.

Allosaurus teeth had zig-zag edges to saw through flesh.

Allosaurus stood on its strong back legs and ran very fast after its prey. It had big jaws, sharp teeth and long claws to strip the meat from its victim.

SPOTLIGHT: Allosaurus

Size:	up to 12 m long
Habitat:	grasslands and forest
Food:	other dinosaurs
Lived:	155–144 million years ago

Armour-plated dinosaur

Stegosaurus was like a walking tank. It was about the same size as Allosaurus but it walked on four legs. It had bony studs to protect its neck, hard plates along its back and spines on its tail.

Stegosaurus ate plants, so it did not need sharp teeth or claws. If a meat-eater attacked, Stegosaurus swung its tail and smashed the hunter with its spines!

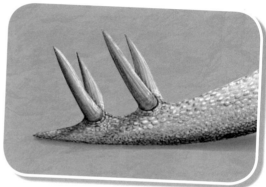

Stegosaurus had sharp spines on its tail.

SPOTLIGHT: Stegosaurus

Size:	about 9 m long and 4 m tall
Habitat:	woods
Food:	moss, ferns, conifers
Lived:	156–140 million years ago

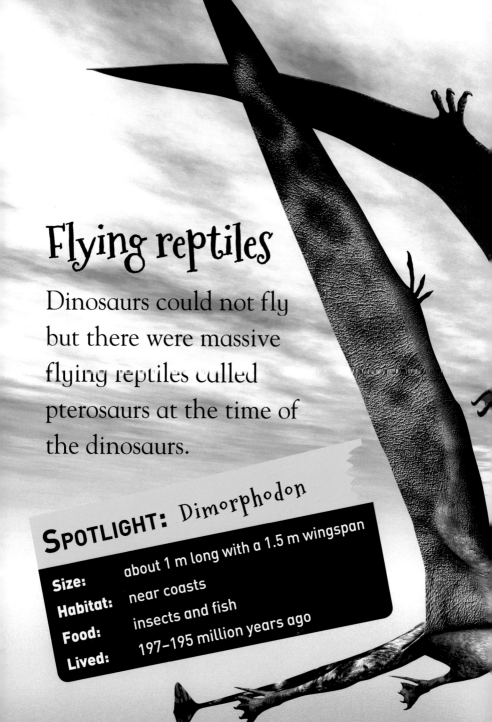

Flying reptiles

Dinosaurs could not fly
but there were massive
flying reptiles called
pterosaurs at the time of
the dinosaurs.

SPOTLIGHT: Dimorphodon

Size: about 1 m long with a 1.5 m wingspan

Habitat: near coasts

Food: insects and fish

Lived: 197–195 million years ago

Pterosaurs had wings made of skin and were the first bony animals to fly.
A pterosaur caught insects in its mouth as it flew through the air.

Dimorphodon was a pterosaur with lots of sharp teeth.

Duckbill dinosaurs

Duckbill dinosaurs were plant-eating dinosaurs. They lived in herds near rivers. The dinosaurs called to each other with booms, honks or squeaks.

Parasaurolophus

The crests of duckbill dinosaurs came in different colours and shapes.

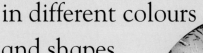

FACT...

Each herd had a different crest on their heads and a different skin pattern too.

SPOTLIGHT: Parasaurolophus

Size:	about 10 m long
Habitat:	rivers, lakes and coasts
Food:	pine needles, leaves, twigs and ferns
Lived:	76–65 million years ago

Baby duckbills

Most (maybe all) dinosaurs laid eggs.
Duckbill dinosaurs called Maiasaura
made their nests in the sand by
rivers and lakes.

Baby Maiasaura were very small when they hatched. When they were big enough to walk, the herd would leave the sandy beach to look for food. The herd would return to the same beach to lay eggs the next year.

Maiasaura egg

SPOTLIGHT: Maiasaura

Size:	about 9 m long
Habitat:	by rivers and lakes
Food:	leaves, berries, seeds and ferns
Lived:	80–65 million years ago

Terrible claws!

Deinonychus was a dangerous meat-eater with sharp curving teeth. It had claws on its hands and feet. One special claw on each foot was long and curved to cut and slash its prey.

SPOTLIGHT: Deinonychus

Size:	up to 3 m long
Habitat:	swamps and forests
Food:	meat
Lived:	115–108 million years ago

Deinonychus were fast runners and hunted in packs. Together, they killed big duckbills and other plant-eating dinosaurs.

Deinonychus's curved claw was 13 centimetres long!

A pack of Deinonychus attack a big plant-eater.

The king

Tyrannosaurus rex was one of the biggest meat-eaters of its time. It had a massive head and strong jaws that could crush bone.

Tyrannosaurus rex had big powerful legs and could run very fast, but it had very small arms. It would track its prey, then charge at it and grab it in its jaws.

SPOTLIGHT: Tyrannosaurus rex

Size: about 12 m long
Habitat: warm forests, near rivers and swamps
Food: meat
Lived: 85–65 million years ago

FACT...

The tooth of a Tyrannosaurus rex has been found buried in the back of a plant-eating Hadrosaur.

This Tyrannosaurus rex tooth is 30 centimetres long.

21

Sea monsters

Dinosaurs lived on land, but at the same time vast sea monsters swam in the ocean.

Megalodon was a prehistoric shark three times bigger than a great white shark. Liopleurodon was a reptile with three-metre-long jaws.

Liopleurodon

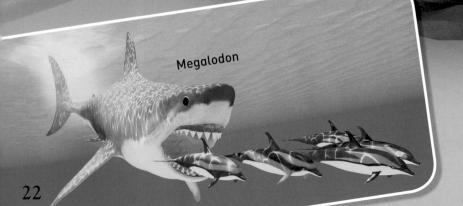

Megalodon

Sarcosuchus was the largest-ever crocodile.

FACT...

Sharks lived in the oceans for millions of years before the dinosaurs – and for millions of years afterwards.

The end

Dinosaurs lived on Earth until they died out quite suddenly 65 million years ago. At this time something terrible happened on Earth that wiped out all the dinosaurs, pterosaurs and the large sea reptiles. Probably a large asteroid hit the Earth and created dust and huge floods.

When the asteroid hit, so much dust went up into the sky that it was winter for many years on Earth.

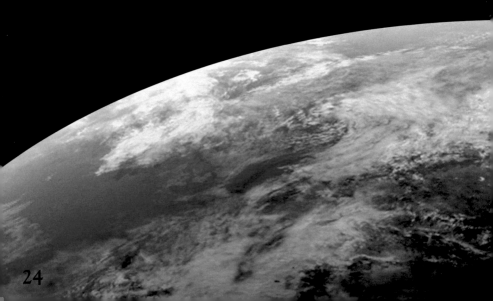

Morganucodon is an early mammal that lived during the late Triassic period.

FACT...

Small animals survived the asteroid event. When the dinosaurs died out, mammals and birds took over the Earth.

Dinosaur hunt

Although dinosaurs are extinct we find out about them from the fossils that are left behind.

These scientists have found a fossilized dinosaur.

Fossils are made over millions of years. The remains of a dinosaur are buried, and sand and mud press down on them. The spaces where the bones were fill with minerals and become rocks in the shape of bones – we call these fossils.

A dinosaur dies by a river. It becomes covered with mud and sand.

The sand and mud protect the remains from the wind and weather. The remains become fossils.

The rock made from sand and mud is worn away by wind and water. The fossils can now be seen.

At the museum

Sometimes scientists find a complete dinosaur skeleton. The skeleton shows the size of an animal, what it looked like and what it ate. It does not show what colour it was or what sounds it made.

This Tyrannosaurus rex skeleton is in the American Museum of Natural History.

Scientists have found fossilized dinosaur footprints. These footprints show how an animal stood and moved. They show if it lived alone or with others in a herd.

a fossilized dinosaur footprint

You can see the bony plates along the back of this Stegosaurus skeleton.

GLOSSARY

asteroid A piece of rock from space.

conifer A tree that grows cones, such as a pine tree.

era A period of time in the past.

extinct No longer living on the Earth.

fern A green plant that has no flowers.

fossil A part of a plant or animal that has turned to stone.

herd A group of animals that live together.

minerals Rock-like substances that are dissolved in water. Minerals replace the bones of a dinosaur to make fossils.

pack A group of animals that hunt together.

plate A hard, flat bit of horn or bone that protects an animal's body.

prey Animals hunted by others for food.

pterosaur A flying reptile that lived at the same time as dinosaurs.

reptile A cold-blooded animal with bones, which often has scales and lays eggs.

spine A sharp, pointed bit of horn or bone.

stud A small, hard bit of horn or bone.

swamp A boggy area.

INDEX

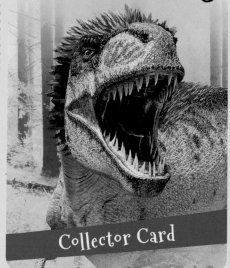

DEADLY
DINOSAURS

Collector Card

DEADLY
DINOSAURS

Collector Card

DEADLY
DINOSAURS

Collector Card

DEADLY
DINOSAURS

Collector Card

Liopleurodon

A top ocean predator with a skull measuring up to 1.5 metres.

SCORE

LENGTH: 7 m	6
DANGER RATING:	9
FOSSIL RECORD: head and bones only	1
WEIGHT: 1500 kg	3

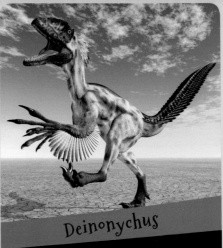

Deinonychus

This dinosaur used a 'terrible claw' to attack its prey.

SCORE

LENGTH: 3 m	2
DANGER RATING:	6
FOSSIL RECORD: only part skeletons	2
WEIGHT: 75 kg	1

Maiasaura

The name of this dinosaur means 'good mother lizard'.

SCORE

LENGTH: 9 m	6
DANGER RATING:	1
FOSSIL RECORD: over 200 specimens	10
WEIGHT: 2500 kg	4

Tyrannosaurus rex

The 'tyrant lizard king' was one of the fiercest animals ever to have lived.

SCORE

LENGTH: 12 m	8
DANGER RATING:	10
FOSSIL RECORD: 20 almost complete	10
WEIGHT: 7000 kg	7

Collect all the titles in this series!

BEASTLY **BUGS**
FREE Collector Cards and Downloadable Audio!

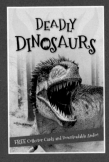

DEADLY **DINOSAURS**
FREE Collector Cards and Downloadable Audio!

FREEZING **POLES**
FREE Collector Cards and Downloadable Audio!

RIOTOUS **RAINFOREST**
FREE Collector Cards and Downloadable Audio!

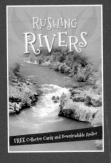

RUSHING **RIVERS**
FREE Collector Cards and Downloadable Audio!

SCARY **SPIDERS**
FREE Collector Cards and Downloadable Audio!

SNAPPY **SHARKS**
FREE Collector Cards and Downloadable Audio!

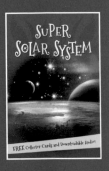

SUPER **SOLAR SYSTEM**
FREE Collector Cards and Downloadable Audio!

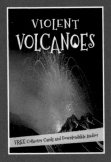

VIOLENT **VOLCANOES**
FREE Collector Cards and Downloadable Audio!

WILD **WEATHER**
FREE Collector Cards and Downloadable Audio!